Tricky, Sneaky Puzzle Pictures

Tricky, Sneaky Puzzle Pictures

Doug Anderson

Sterling Publishing Co., Inc.
New York

Published by Sterling Publishing Company, Inc.
387 Park Avenue South, New York, N.Y. 10016
Originally published under the title *Eye Spy*
© 1980 by Sterling Publishing Company, Inc.
Distributed in Canada by Sterling Publishing
℅ Canadian Manda Group, One Atlantic Avenue, Suite 105
Toronto, Ontario, Canada M6K 3E7
Distributed in Great Britain and Europe by Cassell PLC
Wellington House, 125 Strand, London WC2R 0BB, England
Distributed in Australia by Capricorn Link (Australia) Pty Ltd.
P.O. Box 6651 Baulkham Hills, Business Centre, NSW 2153, Australia

10   9   8   7   6   5   4   3   2

Sterling ISBN 0-8069-9608-0

CONTENTS

To Glinda Harris

HOW TO USE THIS BOOK

The picture puzzles in this book call for a sharp eye and good memory. Sometimes you'll need to note quickly all the details in a picture and recall them later. Sometimes you'll need to find hidden messages or shapes or meanings. Sometimes you'll be able to figure out what's happening from a series of visual clues. And so—in one way or another—these puzzles will help you to develop your powers of observation, memory and deduction.

Many of the puzzles have been given a time limit, and under the picture (or on the following page) are questions for you to answer. Keep a pencil and paper handy, along with a watch or clock for timing yourself. Or a friend could time you and check your final score. You could do the same for him or her, and then compare scores to see who wins. Answers are in the back of the book.

Are these the world's best picture puzzles? We think so. Of course, we don't pretend to know what picture puzzles are like in China or Ghana or Antarctica. But we don't think you'll find a better "Jack-the-Ripper Fan Club" puzzle—or a better "Hello Dali" puzzle—or a "Can-Can" puzzle that compares with the one in this book. (Actually, we'd be very surprised if you found another "Jack-the-Ripper Fan Club" or "Hello Dali" or "Can-Can" puzzle anywhere!) But whether these are the world's best picture puzzles or not, we hope you'll find them challenging and fun.

Ready? Get set!

1. GET SET!

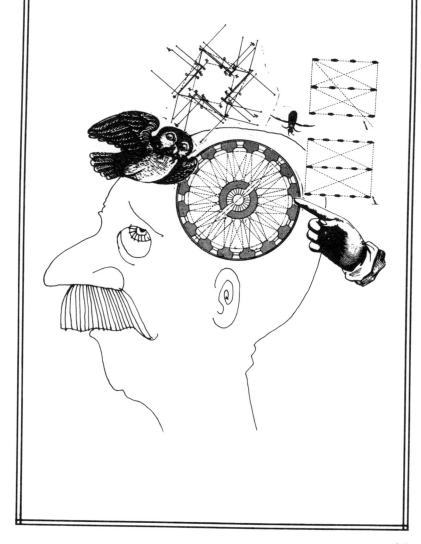

The World's Best Birds-in-the-Hand Puzzle

How many birds can you count in thirty seconds?

Answer on page 120.

The World's Best Dinohooper Puzzle

These are Dinohoopers.

These are NOT Dinohoopers.

Mr. J.   **Miss S.**   **Miss H.**   **Mr. R.**

Which of these are Dinohoopers?

Answer on page 120.

13

The World's Best Mixed-Up Menagerie Puzzle

These crazy creatures are very mixed up. They are actually made up of the parts of seven animals. Can you unscramble them? (*1 minute*)

Answer on page 120.

The World's Best Wanted Man Puzzle

WANTED!

JAMES JONES (*alias "Mugsy"*)
Age: 37   *Height:* 6'7"
Weight: 176   *Hair:* Black
Eyes: One blue, one brown.
Jones has a scar on his right cheek,
a bird tattoo on his right arm, and is
missing a finger on his left hand.

James "Mugsy" Jones was elected "Most Wanted Man of the Year" by *Preyboy Magazine*. Study this wanted poster for thirty seconds. Then turn the page.

The World's Best
Wanted Man Puzzle *(continued)*

They've caught him! Well, maybe they've caught him. Which of the suspects in the line-up is the "Most Wanted Man"? Is any one of them?

Answer on page 120.

The World's Best Can-Can Puzzle

The items on these pages all have "can" in their names. How many can you identify in a minute?

Answer on page 120.

The World's Best Missing Earring Puzzle

Mrs. Vanderposh, the world's richest woman, has just realized that one of her most precious jewels— a diamond earring—is missing. It looks exactly like the one she's wearing. Has someone snatched it? Or can you find it in her jewel box? (*1 minute*)

Answer on page 120.

The World's Best
Strange Handwriting Puzzle

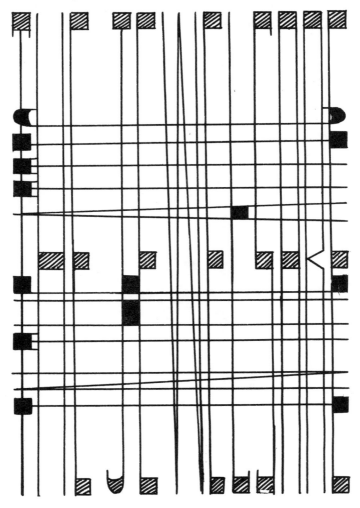

Celestine, the cat burglar, decided to go straight. She left this message for the police, but out of habit, she wrote it in code. Can you decode it in a minute?

Answer on page 120.

The World's Best
Bad Speller Puzzle

"Three Fingers" spent so much time in a life of crime that he never did learn how to spell. When he had to write a letter to his partner, he used pictures from newspapers and magazines for most of the words. You have one minute to figure out his message.

Answer on page 120.

The World's Best
Stupid
Get-Away Car
Puzzle

If you were going to use a car to commit a crime, you wouldn't be likely to choose this one. But it was found parked near the scene of the crime. Study it for a minute. Then turn the page.

The World's Best
Stupid Get-Away Car Puzzle

(continued)

1. What state is the car from?
2. What is its license number?
3. Describe the ornament on the hood.
4. What is the monogram on the door?
5. What is tied to the radio antenna?
6. Was anything left in the car?
7. What does the sign on the windshield say?
8. Are the tires new?

Answer on page 120.

2. SLYJINX

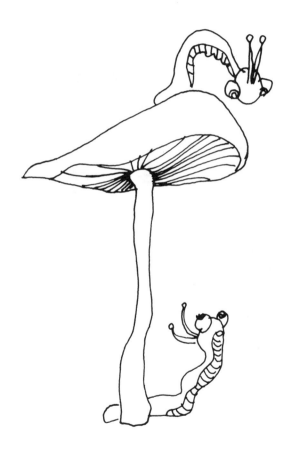

The World's Best
Frank the Forger Puzzle

Frank the Forger tried to copy the masterpiece marked A. Alas, he left out some details and he couldn't resist adding others that were not in the original. Can you spot the mistakes in his creation—painting B?

Answers on page 120.

The World's Best Elusive Man Puzzle

You are tailing a suspect. He is a male, about thirty years old, with a moustache. When last seen, he was wearing a hat, bow tie, and was carrying some papers. Can you spot him in thirty seconds?

The World's Best Elusive Man Puzzle (continued)

Answers on page 120.

The World's Best Hidden Vampire Puzzle

Count Dracula rented a castle to use until his condo is ready. Could this be the one? Go up the path, if you dare, and peek in the window . . . .

The World's Best
Hidden Vampire Puzzle

Can you find the Drac himself, his pal Igor and his administrative assistant? (*2 minutes*)

Answer on page 121.

The World's Best Turnaround Puzzle

This is more a test of your imagination than a puzzle. The more you look at these diagrams, the more pictures you'll see. Turn each picture four ways, use your imagination and give each one a title. Your friends may see them entirely differently than you do. No time limit on this one.

Possible answers on page 121.

The World's Best Polypod Puzzle

These are Polypods.

These are NOT Polypods.

| Jasper | Marylee | Gramps | Lenny |

Which of these are Polypods?

Answer on page 121.

The World's Best Handle Puzzle

Can you name the items that these handles were taken from? (*1 minute*)

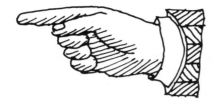

Answer on page 121.

The World's Best Fingerprint Matching Puzzle

This jumble of fingerprints was found at the scene of the crime. Does one of them belong to the arch criminal Evil Evan? That's his print, under the magnifying glass. But the computers are down and it may be hours before you'll be able to have it checked. Can you match Evan's print to any of the ones in the jumble?

The World's Best Fingerprint Matching Puzzle (continued)

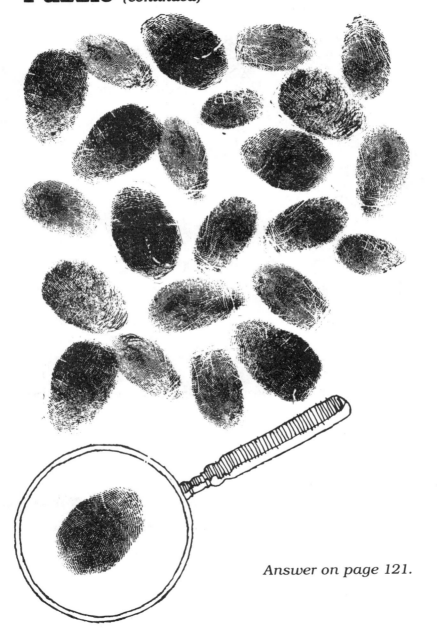

Answer on page 121.

3. EYE TO EYE

The World's Best Mad Hatter Puzzle

Mrs. Timbuck

Mrs. Timbuck bought a very expensive hat. Mrs. Tew tried to copy it exactly. But has she?

Compare the hats for one minute and see how many differences you can find.

Mrs. Tew

Answer on page 121.

The World's Best Buggy Puzzle

Study these pages for two minutes.
1. How many of the butterflies are exactly alike?
2. What in the picture is *not* a bug or a butterfly?
3. What is impossible about one of the butterflies?

Answers on page 121-122.

The World's Best Which-Two-Are-Not-Like-the-Others Puzzle

Of these ten objects, eight have something in common. What? Which two do not fit in? (*1 minute*)

Answer on page 122.

The World's Best Masquerade Hat Puzzle

Seven guests are at the masquerade. Can you tell from the hats what characters they are impersonating? (*1 minute*)

Answers on page 122.

The World's Best Tracks-Making Puzzle

Study these people for a minute. Then turn the page.

The World's Best Tracks-Making Puzzle

(continued)

Which one made these tracks?

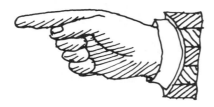

Answer on page 122.

The World's Best Cityscape Puzzle

In this city, many items start with the letter S. How many can you find? (*3 minutes*)

Now how many can you find that begin with the letter B? (*2 minutes*)

Answers on page 122.

The World's Best Split Personality Puzzles

Both of these charmers have split personalities. Somewhere inside them is another complete entity. Can you find it? (*1 minute*)

Answers on page 122.

4. OOOOPS!

The World's Best Defective Merchandise Puzzle

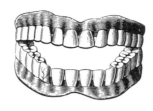

All the merchandise on these pages is being returned for a refund. Can you detect the flaw in each one? (*1 minute*)

Answers on page 122.

The World's Best Lost Legs Puzzle

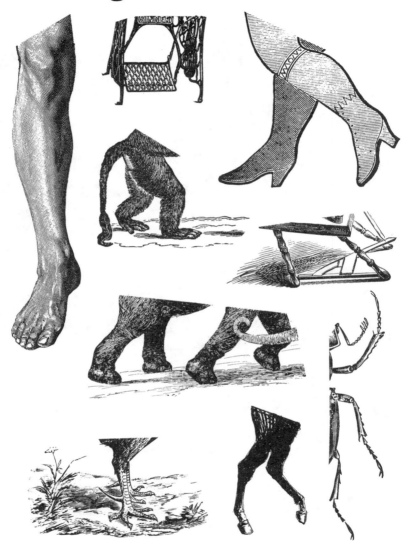

Can you tell who—or what—owns these legs? (*1 minute*)

Answers on page 122.

The World's Best Monster Mix & Match Puzzle

Magda Monster

Answer on page 123.

Magda Monster and her friends on the next two pages were made up of odd bits and pieces that Dan, the Demented Doctor, found lying around his laboratory. Spend a minute on each page and see if you can list the ingredients Dan used in each monster.

The World's Best Monster Puzzle
Mix & Match
(continued)

Monster Musician

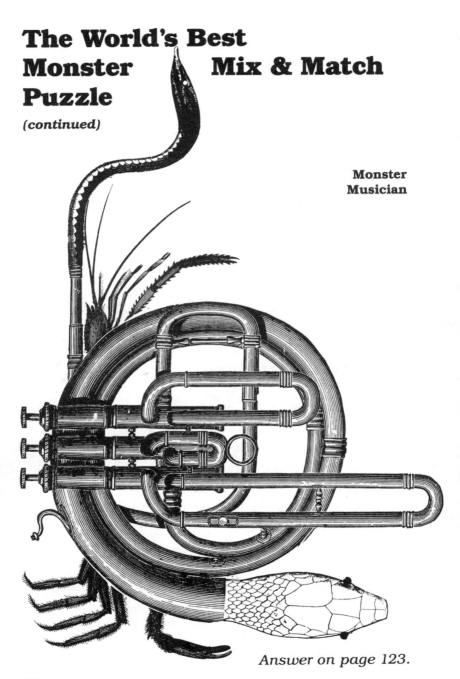

Answer on page 123.

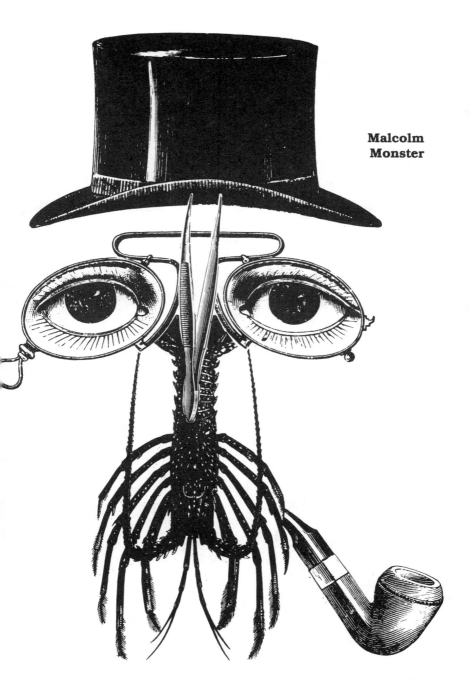

Malcolm
Monster

The World's Best
Ghastly Garden Puzzle

They say that Old Mr. Tumbleweed keeps ghastly things in his garden, though no one is willing to guess what.

How many ghastly things can you find? (*1 minute*)

Answer on page 123.

The World's Best
Sloppy Sign Painter Puzzle

Sam the Sign Painter took on more work than he had time for. Also, he is a slob. So it's not surprising that he's going to have to do many of these signs all over again tomorrow. Which signs is he going to have to repaint? (*2 minutes*)

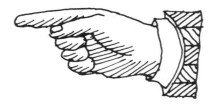

Answer on page 123.

The World's Best Stay-on-the-Line Puzzle

Woody, Captain Bill, Lana, Alex and Mr. Parker all like to fish, but are they in for a surprise! Turn the page. You have two minutes to tell who will catch what when the lines are pulled in.

The World's Best Stay-on-the-Line Puzzle

Woody **Captain Bill** **Lana** **Alex** **Mr. Parker**

Answers on page 123.

5. SNEAKS

The World's Best Terrible Twins Puzzle

When the supermarket was robbed, the police recognized the MO of the Terrible Twins. The twins tried to get lost in the crowd. Can you find them in one minute?

Answer on page 123.

The World's Second Best Turnaround Puzzle

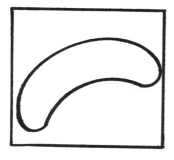

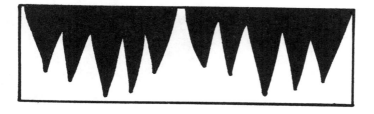

As in the puzzle on page 34, this is more a test of your imagination than a puzzle. Turn the book around, look at each diagram from every angle, see what it looks like and give it a name. The more names for each diagram, the better your score. No time limit on this one.

Possible answers on page 123.

65

The World's Best Monster Rally Puzzle

The Head Ghoul has called a rally. All the uglies are to meet at midnight in the swamp and bring their

own lunch. Study this pesky parade for one minute and see how many monsters are on their way.

Answer on page 124.

The World's Best Useless Machine Puzzle

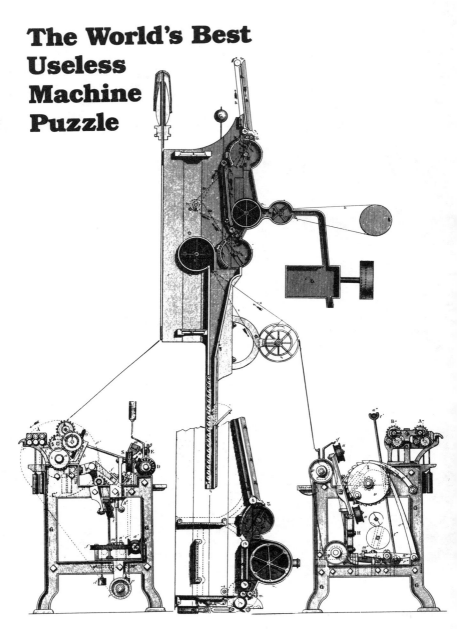

Mr. Fix-it invented this interesting machine. It doesn't work, but it looks good.

Mr. Copicat tried to make one exactly like it, but his spies forgot to tell him about four parts. Can you tell which parts are missing in one minute?

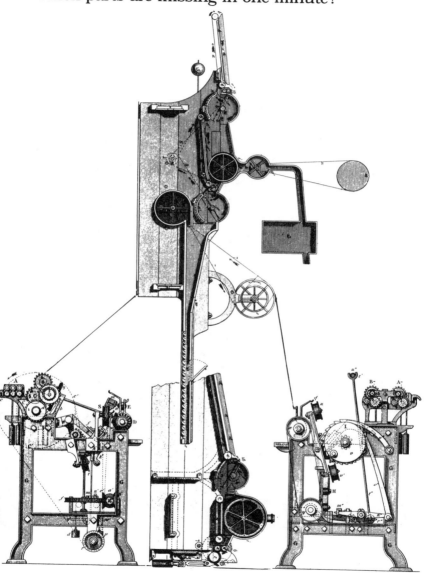

Answer on page 124.

The World's Best Animals-on-the-Loose Puzzle

Several animals escaped from the zoo and managed to hide in the bushes of this tropical park. They are apt to annoy the tourists. How many are here? What are they? Can you find them in thirty seconds?

Answer on page 124.

The World's Best Mystery Word Puzzle

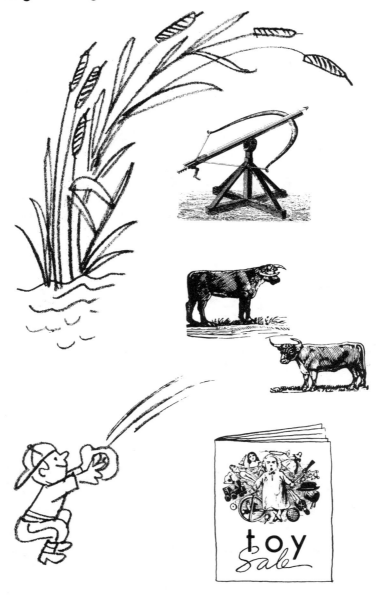

Each item on these pages has the same three-letter word in its name. What is the word? Can you identify every picture in two minutes?

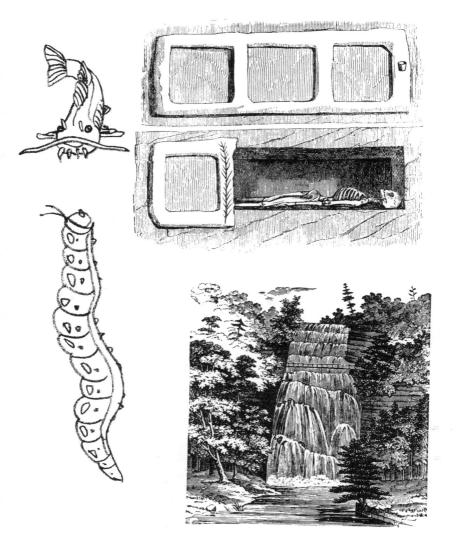

Answer on page 124.

The World's Best Secret Plans Puzzle

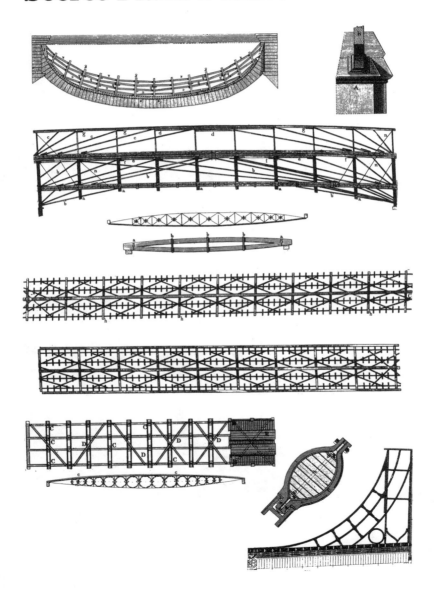

Professor Moriarty has once again outwitted the police and disappeared with the crown jewels. But wait! He burned something before he left, and he missed a few scraps of paper. They may tell where the jewels are hidden. They seem to be plans—but what are they for? A railroad track? A bridge? A fence? A cathedral? (*1 minute*)

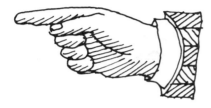

Answer on page 124.

The World's Best Jack-the-Ripper Fan Club Puzzle

The members of the Jack-the-Ripper Fan Club have gone underground, and no one knows how many of them are still around. This picture is said to show the entire JTRF club. How many are there? (*1 minute*)

The World's Best Jack-the-Ripper Fan Club Puzzle *(continued)*

Answer on page 124.

6. CLOSE ENCOUNTERS

The World's Best Extraterrestrial Invasion Puzzle

The UFO landed for a moment in the garden of the Embassy. Before it took off, some of its passengers hid in the trees.

The Ambassador isn't fooled. He sensed immediately that extraterrestrials were present and believes he spotted five of them. How many can you find? (*2 minutes*)

Answer on page 124.

The World's Best Alien Beast Puzzle

Mr. and Mrs. Em, along with son Ernie, were working late one night at their printing press. Suddenly, an unpleasant beast from Krypton arrived on the scene. The Ems, all three of them, hid. Can you find them? (*2 minutes*)

Answers on page 124.

The World's Best
Two from Taurus Puzzle

All Taureans do not dress alike. In this regiment of typical Taureans, only one pair are dressed exactly the same. Which ones? (*2 minutes*)

Answer on page 125.

The World's Best Tail-Disappearing Puzzle

Every night for nine nights, Mrs. Queazy thought she heard someone—or something—in her back yard. Each night she ran to the window just in time to see (or so she imagined) a different tail-end disappearing over the fence. Here are sketches of what she saw, as she described them to a police department artist. Can you identify Mrs. Queazy's intruders? (*2 minutes*)

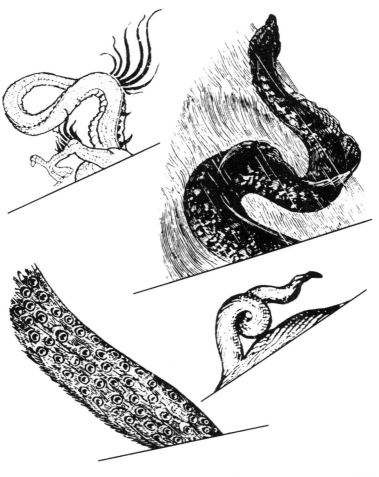

Answer on page 125.

The World's Best Absurd Bird Puzzle

Birds of a feather stick together, but this bird is stuck together from the parts of four birds. Can you name them? (*1 minute*)

Answer on page 125.

7. TIME FLIES

The World's Best Unlocked Window Puzzle

This quiet living room contains several valuable antiques. This is how it looked before the burglar came.

The same living room four hours later. See if you can discover what was stolen.

After one minute, turn the page.

The World's Best Unlocked Window Puzzle (continued)

One of these odd-looking people is the burglar.

Which one would you arrest?

Answer on page 125.

The World's Best Trip Home Puzzle

1

2

3

After a hard day's work, Mr. Bome is headed for home at 106 Jane Lane. Can you help him on his way by putting the five pictures in their correct order? (*1 minute*)

4

5

Answer on page 125.

The World's Best
Best-of-Times Puzzle

Take two minutes to study these timepieces. Then turn the page.

The World's Best Best-of-Times Puzzle

(continued)

Can you tell:
1. How many clocks are in the picture?
2. How many watches are in the picture?
3. How many of the timepieces are exactly on the hour?
4. How many have Roman numerals?
5. How many have second hands?
6. What is wrong with one of the clocks?

Answers on page 125.

8. LOOKING SHARP

The World's Best Nameless Monster Puzzle

Colonel Mustard created this monster, but can't think of a name for it. If you identify the five items used to make the monster, the first letter of each item will spell out a name. (*2 minutes*)

Answer on page 125.

The World's Best Old Plans Puzzle

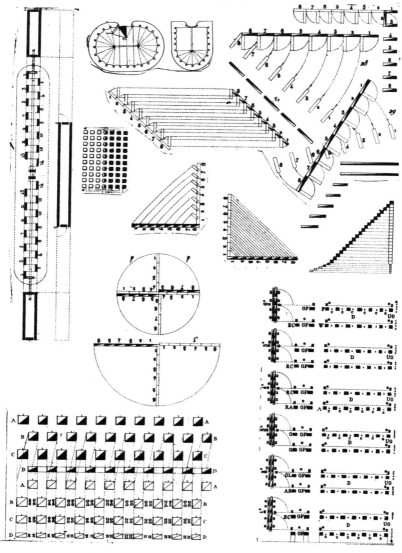

These plans were found in an old trunk. Study them for one minute. Then turn the page.

The World's Best
Old Plans Puzzle (continued)

Who was the creator of these plans?
A city planner?
An architect?
A sports promoter?
A general?

Answer on page 125.

The World's Best
Too-Many-Shoes Puzzle

Emma has so many shoes that she can never find a matching pair. So most of the time she goes barefoot. Can you solve Emma's dilemma and let her know how many complete pairs of shoes she actually has? (*1 minute*)

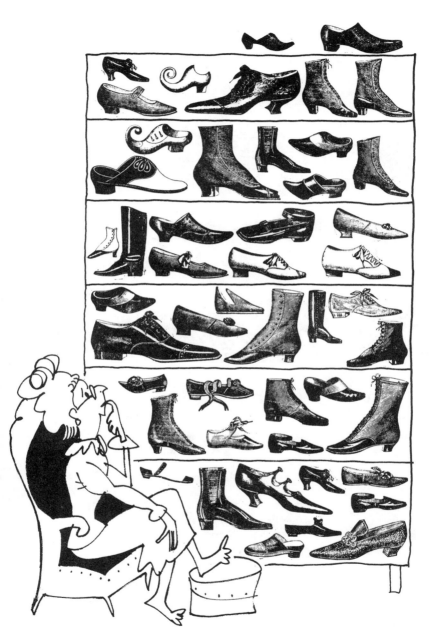

Answer on page 125.

The World's Best Beeline Puzzle

 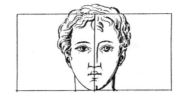

Each bee starts a different word that begins *BE* . . . .
How many of these "bee lines" can you decipher in
one minute?

Answers on page 125.

The World's Best Forgetful General Puzzle

He may be a military genius, but he can't keep track of his stars. He doesn't even remember how many he has. Can you help him find them all? (*2 minutes*)

Answer on page 126.

The World's Best Christmas Present Puzzle

There is something in the Christmas picture on the next page that starts with each letter of the alphabet. How many can you list in five minutes? (*Hint:* You may call an item by more than one name. For example, a "Drum" can also be a "Toy.") (*3 minutes*)

The World's Best Christmas Present Puzzle

(continued)

Answers on page 126.

9. GENIUS AT PLAY

The World's Best
Tools-of-the-Trade Puzzle

 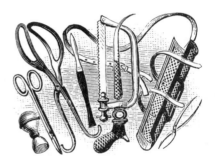

Every one of these old lithographs shows the tools needed for a different trade or old-time craft. Can you name them? (*2 minutes*)

Answers on page 126.

The World's Best Asterisk Cover-Up Puzzle

Can you figure out which commonly used phrases are listed below? Each asterisk stands for a letter, and you can use any word that is pictured in the drawings on the next page. For example, one of the phrases might be: **** in the ****

The answer could be BIRD in the HAND. (*3 minutes*)

1. **** out of *****
2. ****** in *****
3. ****** *** into the ****
4. **** in ***
5. ****** in ***** ******
6. **** in the ****
7. ***** on ******
8. ***** of a *******
9. a ***** in ****
10. ******* in your ***
11. *** in a ***
12. *** in ****
13. *** the ****
14. *** in the ****

Answers on page 126.

a line

2

1

111

The World's Best Hello Dali Puzzle

The artist has incorporated at least five related elements in this painting. Can you come up with an appropriate title? (*1 minute*)

Answer on page 126.

The World's Best Do-It-Yourself Puzzle

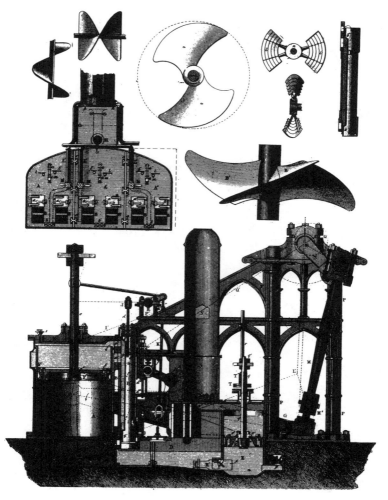

Rich Mr. Critch bought these expensive parts to build something in his spare time. Then he forgot what he was going to build. Can you tell him? (*1 minute*)

Answer on page 126.

The World's Best
Fish-Counting Puzzle

How many fishes can you count in two minutes?

Answer on page 126.

The World's Best Robogrumpet Puzzle

These are Robogrumpets.

These are NOT Robogrumpets.

| Tammy | Tor | Bruce | Eleanora |

Which of these are Robogrumpets?

Answer on page 126.

The World's Best Round-the-Block Puzzle

They're off! Or they will be if they ever reach the starting line. Study these crazy racers for one minute. Then turn the page to see who won.

The World's Best Round-the-Block Puzzle

(continued)

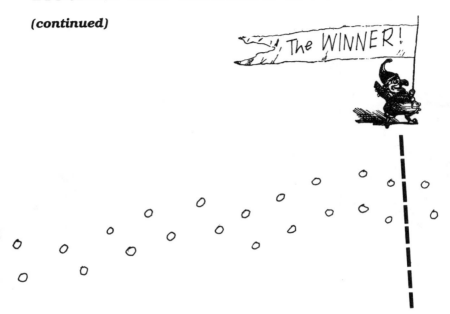

Only one racer got all the way around the block. All the others dropped out. Can you tell by the tracks who won?

Answer on page 126.

ANSWERS

Answers

1. GET SET!

The World's Best Birds-in-the-Hand Puzzle

17.

The World's Best Dinohooper Puzzle

Mr. J. is not a Dinohooper.
Miss S. is a Dinohopper.
Miss H. is a Dinohooher.
Mr. R. is not a Dinohopper.

All Dinohoopers have two legs and a curly tail.

The World's Best Mixed-Up Menagerie Puzzle

Top: Lion, Zebra
Middle: Rhinoceros, Hyena
Bottom: Camel, Giraffe, Kangaroo

The World's Best Wanted Man Puzzle

The third man from the left is Mugsy.

The World's Best Can-Can Puzzle

Cantaloupe	Canvas
Canoe	Candidate
Canteen	Canopy
Candy cane	Cannon
Candelabra	Canary
Candle	Toucan

The World's Best Missing Earring Puzzle

The missing earring is at the lower right-hand corner of the jewel box.

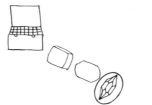

The World's Best Strange Handwriting Puzzle

Hold the page flat at eye level and rotate slowly from left to right. Then turn the page from vertical to horizontal. The message reads: THE JEWELS ARE IN THE ATTIC.

The World's Best Bad Speller Puzzle

Dear Swanson: Be at the corner today at five o'clock. Bring the booty. Keep your cut and leave mine.

(signed) Three Fingers Fisher

The World's Best Stupid Get-Away Car Puzzle

1. Ohio
2. 27941
3. A horse
4. dhc
5. A balloon
6. A guitar
7. "No radio"
8. No, two of the tires are patched.

2. SLYJINX

The World's Best Frank the Forger Puzzle

Frank made nine mistakes, which are circled.

The World's Best Elusive Man Puzzle

The man you are after is third from the left in the second row.

The World's Best Hidden Vampire Puzzle

Turn the picture upside down. Now, on the left-hand page, you'll see Dracula in the center of the picture at the bottom. Keep the picture upside down and find Igor on the left, behind the tassel. Dracula's administrative assistant is on the right, her face in the wings of the large bat.

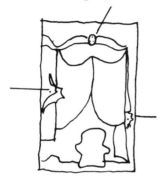

The World's Best Turnaround Puzzle

Below, a few possibilities for titles.

Top left: Lobster claw, Bird's beak, Rhino's tail, Shark

Top right: Dove, Canoe, Swallowing a grape, Hole-in-one

Center: Waves, Dragon's teeth, Saw blade, Christmas tree

Bottom Left: Owl, Table and stools, Moons over a mountain, Fish

Bottom Right: Crow's foot, Broken ice, Party hat, Lily

The World's Best Polypod Puzzle

Jasper is not a Polypod.
Marylee is not a Polypod.
Gramps is not a Polypod.
Lenny is a Polypod.

All Polypods have six spots and a nostril.

The World's Best Handle Puzzle

A sword
Brooms
A shovel
A watch
A faucet
A pump
A spade
A pliers
A saw
A wheelbarrow

The World's Best Fingerprint Matching Puzzle

The matching print is second from the right in the third row from the top.

3. EYE TO EYE

The World's Best Mad Hatter Puzzle

Mrs. Tew's hat is missing one butterfly and a beetle.

The World's Best Buggy Puzzle

1. Two butterflies only are exactly alike. They look like this:

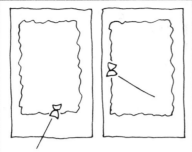

2. The acorn is not a bug or a butterfly.
3. The butterfly in the center of the top row (left-hand page) has only one wing.

The World's Best Which-Two-Are-Not-Like-the-Others Puzzle

They all have legs—except the snake and the star.

The World's Best Masquerade Hat Puzzle

A clown
A gentleman
Mercury
A knight
A king
An explorer
A European general

The World's Best Tracks-Making Puzzle

The man with the wheelbarrow.

The World's Best Cityscape Puzzle

Sailboat	Shoes	Skylight
Sailor	Shoe store	Skyscrapers
Sea	Sidewalk	Stairs
Seagulls	Sign	Steeple
Settee	Sky	Subway
Seller (of balloons)	Sun	

Ball	Birds	Boy
Balloons	Boat	Building
Bank	Books	Bus
Banner	Book store	

The World's Best Split Personality Puzzle

(*Left*) Turn the picture upside down and the other self emerges. (*Right*) Study her nose. This sketch will help.

4. OOOOPS!

The World's Best Defective Merchandise Puzzle

One tooth is cracked.
The flame is missing from the torch of the Statue of Liberty.
The chair has only three legs.
The watch has two 9's.
The microscope is missing the holder for the specimen.
One rung is missing from the stepladder.
The pitcher has a broken handle.
The bicycle's seat is upside down.

The World's Best Lost Legs Puzzle

A man
A sewing machine
A doll
A monkey
A spinning wheel
An elephant
A rooster
A horse
A beetle

The World's Best Monster Mix & Match Puzzle

MAGDA MONSTER:
A rooster's tail
A wig
A beetle's legs
A tooth
A peacock's tail
Eyeglasses (with eyes)

MONSTER MUSICIAN:
Heads of two snakes
A lobster's legs
A French horn

MALCOLM MONSTER:
A top hat
Eyeglasses (with eyes)
A lobster
Tweezers
A pipe

The World's Best Ghastly Garden Puzzle

On the right-hand page is a disembodied hand and a skull. (There is also a snake, which you may not consider "ghastly.") On the left-hand page is a man's head and a floating foot.

The World's Best Sloppy Sign Painter Puzzle

There is at least one mistake on every one of Sam's signs. The signs should read:

Cafeteria Open
Do Not Disturb
No Smoking
Deer Crossing
Thru Traffic
Rest Stop Ahead

The Stop and Yield signs should have their shapes transposed. The speed sign should read 15 M.P.H. *Additional errors:* The Railroad sign contains a backwards R. The N in the word "SIGNS" on the window is backwards. The Right Turn sign also has a backwards N, as well as an arrow pointing in the wrong direction. Both "One Way" signs point in both directions.

The World's Best Stay-on-the-Line Puzzle

Woody: A shoe
Captain Bill: An autochair
Lana: A peculiar fish
Alex: A crab
Mr. Parker: A machine

5. SNEAKS

The World's Best Terrible Twins Puzzle

The twins are the harmless-looking gentlemen in glasses in the upper left and low center.

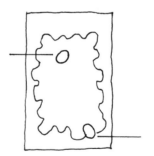

The World's Second Best Turnaround Puzzle

Below, a few possibilities for titles.
Top left: Sausage, Boomerang, Clown's smile, Swimming pool
Top right: Vase, Doorknob, Keyhole, Bicycle horn
Center: Claws, School of fish, Icicles, Banners
Bottom Left: Clown's hat, Fish, Octopus, Moon and clouds
Bottom Right: Hitchhiker, Duck's tail, Thumbprint, Swan

The World's Best Monster Rally Puzzle

There are two monsters in addition to the six you see at once. Turn the book upside down and you will see the face of the seventh monster in the folds of the witch's black sleeve, and an eighth monster on the back of her skirt.

The World's Best Useless Machine Puzzle

Two valves and two wheels are missing from Mr. Copicat's machine.

The World's Best Animals-on-the-Loose Puzzle

Turn the book upside down. There is an elephant, a lion, a snake, a rhinoceros, a lizard and a giraffe.

The World's Best Mystery Word Puzzle

The word is CAT:

Cat-o'-nine tails	Catacomb
Catapult	Catfish
Cattle	Caterpillar
Catalogue	Cataract
Catch	

The World's Best Secret Plans Puzzle

A bridge

The World's Best Jack-the-Ripper Fan Club Puzzle

There are 18 members.

6. CLOSE ENCOUNTERS

The World's Best Extraterrestrial Invasion Puzzle

There are 7 extraterrestrials in the trees. If you find 5, the Ambassador will show you his medals. Find eight and he'll give you one.

The World's Best Alien Beast Puzzle

Mr. and Mrs. Em are on the left-hand page. Their frightened faces are hidden in the machinery. Ernie's face is on the right-hand page (just as scared).

The World's Best Two from Taurus Puzzle

One twin is on the left-hand page, second from the left on the bottom line. The other twin is on the right-hand page, second from the right on the second line.

The World's Best Tail-Disappearing Puzzle

Left-hand page: A horse
                             A comet
                             A fish
                             A devil
                             A rooster

Right-hand page: A dragon
                             An eel
                             A pig
                             A peacock

The World's Best Absurd Bird Puzzle

An eagle
A stork
An ostrich
A peacock

7. TIME FLIES

The World's Best Unlocked Window Puzzle

Stolen were:
The candlestick
The deer's head
A flower
Arrest the gentleman with the cane, top hat, one black glove and the stolen flower in his button hole. He left his other glove on the floor of the living room.

The World's Best Trip Home Puzzle

Order of pictures: 2/3/5/4/1. The clues are the clock, the street numbers, the cat in the window and the matching houses.

The World's Best Best-of-Times Puzzle

1. Six
2. Seven
3. Two
4. Ten
5. Seven
6. The clock on the lower right-hand side of the left page is missing one hand.

8. LOOKING SHARP

The World's Best Nameless Monster Puzzle

B for Barbells
A for Arrow (or Arm)
S for Skull
I for Ivory
L for Lantern or Lamp
The suggested name: Basil.

The World's Best Old Plans Puzzle

A general. These are plans for a military battle.

The World's Best Too-Many-Shoes Puzzle

Emma has only one pair of exactly matching shoes. The shoe in the top left-hand corner and the shoe second from the right in the third row from the bottom are the same.

The World's Best Beeline Puzzle

   Behead
   Betrayal (trail)
   Benign
   Behooves
   Beloved
   Beagle
   Behind
   Begun
   Befoul
   Behemoth
   Bestir
   Beforehand

The World's Best Forgetful General Puzzle

He is a three-star general.

The World's Best Christmas Present Puzzle

Ark	Necklace
Ball	Ornament
Camel	Puppet
Drum	Queen
Engine	Racquet
Fish	Sword
Grapes	Toy
Horn	Umbrella
Ice wagon	Van
Jack-in-the-box	Wagon
Key	Xylophone
Locomotive	Yacht
Monkey	Zebra

9. GENIUS AT PLAY

The World's Best Tools of the Trade Puzzle

Barber
Auctioneer
Carpenter
Surgeon
Upholsterer
Plumber
Cooper
Teacher
Mason
Butcher

The World's Best Asterisk Cover-Up Puzzle

1. Fish out of water
2. Tongue in cheek
3. Frying pan into the fire
4. Hole in one
5. People in glass houses
6. Hole in the wall
7. Right on target
8. Birds of a feather
9. A stitch in time
10. Feather in your cap
11. Bug in a rug
12. Cap in hand
13. Toe the line
14. Two in the bush

The World's Best Hello Dali Puzzle

The artist has painted touch, sight, sound, smell, taste. If you caught onto the idea of the five senses, any corresponding title is an acceptable answer.

The World's Best Do-It-Yourself Puzzle

A steamboat

The World's Best Fish-Counting Puzzle

You should net fourteen fish (the starfish counts). If you counted the octopus, throw him back (he's a mollusk).

The World's Best Robogrumpet Puzzle

Tammy is a Robogrumpet.
Tor is not a Robogrumpet.
Bruce in not a Robogrumpet.
Eleanora is a Robogrumpet.

All Robogrumpets are made up of at least one triangle, one oval and one circle.

The World's Best Round-the-Block Puzzle

The ballerina won.

About the Author

Doug Anderson has illustrated over 70 books—serious and humorous, for adults and for children—since he came from his native New England in 1946 to work as a free-lance artist in New York.

The first drawing he ever sold went to *The New Yorker*, and since then his artwork has appeared in most of the country's major magazines—among them, *Fortune*, *Good Housekeeping*, *Reader's Digest*, *Gourmet*, *Seventeen*, *This Week* and *The New Yorker*—as well as newspapers, including *The New York Times*, *The Boston Globe* and *The Washington Post*.

He has written several books, among them *Eye Spy*, on which this book is based, *New Things to Draw and How to Draw Them*, and *How to Draw with the Light Touch*. For several years he was a monthly contributor to the highly respected *Theatre Arts* magazine, and articles have also appeared under his name in *The New York Times* travel section and in *American Artist* magazine.

Doug lives and works in New York City.

Index